THE
DAD I WISH
I HAD

D1367912

"There is an extraordinary amount of practical wisdom dispensed in this book. You can clearly see God's message regarding the impact a father has on his household both positively and negatively through the eyes of the young people in the camp experience. But Freddie systematically goes beyond the realm of simply identifying the problems by providing God inspired solutions. Read it and you will be blessed."

Jim Caldwell, Head Coach,
Indianapolis Colts

"I was blessed that my father Lowell was the quintessential role model and mentor for me as a boy and as a man. One thing that he instilled in me very early on was that 'you make a living by what you earn, but you make a life by what you give.' This philosophy has served me well as CEO of Big Brothers Big Sisters of Middle Tennessee and how I approach life in general. Freddie's book should be an inspiration to men from all walks of life to demonstrate an attitude of gratitude through service to others, beginning with their own sons."

Lowell Perry, CEO,
Big Brothers Big Sisters of Middle TN

THE
DAD I WISH
I HAD

By
Freddie L. Scott II

Foreward by
Tony Dungy
New York Times Best Selling Author,
"Quiet Strength"

UNLOCK THE CHAMPION

Contents

ACKNOWLEDGEMENTS

"Catching a glimpse of our life from my child's perspective further enlightened me. It was evident to me that I was clueless on the adverse affect of my absence from the home because of my selfishness. Key emotions were realized as I read this book but none greater than love. I could see and feel the love the children had for me during those times and was not understanding of how critical those times were to the family. God's love for us all came across strong in the book and I know that without His love, their mother's effort to keep them worshipping in a good bible teaching church and their personal commitment to follow God, not man, Freddie could have easily become one of the earlier statistics he referenced in the book.

Love you son and thank you for making yourself available to link God to your past and your future - your dad and your own children- as we address the needs of the now/present!

Looking forward to hearing about more speaking engagements and more books!"

Love,
Freddie Scott, Sr. (Dad)

FOREWARD

Our country is facing a crisis right now, but I'm not sure most people recognize it. We're focused on the economy—people are losing jobs, banks are failing, the stock market is falling and our auto manufacturers are looking for help. But the economy is not our biggest problem. We have another threat to our society that is even worse and that is the deterioration of our family structure.

God's plan for the family starts with the father being the spiritual leader, provider and head of the household. In America today, we are moving farther and farther away from that model. Our legal system is trying to make sure that dads are providing financial support for their children, and while that's necessary, it isn't nearly enough. Our kids need the teaching, guidance and love that dads should provide and because they are not getting it, we're seeing a multitude of problems.

Low graduation rates, juvenile arrests, teen pregnancies and just the general dysfunction that we're seeing in our families today can be traced to the absence of fathers in the home. And if we don't change the momentum soon, we may not be able to pull out of this.

I was very fortunate to have my dad around for the first forty nine years of my life. I learned a lot from him and I'm still using many of those lessons today. Not just how to do things that boys need to learn to have fun, like how to throw a ball or ride a bike. But I also learned a lot of things from him about life. I learned why it's important to study and work hard to get good grades. I learned how to control my temper, how to treat other people with respect, how to deal with disappointments as well as successes. And I learned about family—how to treat a wife, how to treat children and how to provide for them. I also got something else because of my dad—access to the rest of his family and a chance to learn things from grandparents, aunts, uncles and cousins.

Today our boys and girls aren't always getting a chance to have these advantages. They're not getting to learn these lessons with the help of a father and the only way that is going to change is if we men do something to break this cycle. Freddie Scott is tackling this issue with "The Dad I Wish I Had." He is not only providing an honest look at the problem but giving sound biblical solutions for overcoming it. I know that reading it will be enlightening and challenging. My hope is that this book inspires you to think about ways we can get our dads back to their rightful place in this country— involved and active in their children's lives.

Tony Dungy

INTRODUCTION

It amazes me that the issues of children and their fathers seem to go unheard. Not having a father in the home seems to be accepted as normal in our society.

The National Center for Fatherless Statistics (www.fathers.com):

According to 72.2 % of the U.S. population, fatherlessness is the most significant family or social problem facing America. Source: National Center for Fathering, Fathering in America Poll, January, 1999.

An estimated 23.6 million children (32.3 percent) live absent their biological father. Source: U.S. Census Bureau. Current Population Survey Reports. "Household Relationship and Living Arrangements of Children Under 18 Years, by Age, Sex, Race, Hispanic Origin: 2004.

Of students in grades 1 through 12, 39 percent (17.7 million) live in homes absent their biological fathers. Source: Nord, Christine Winquist, and Jerry West. Fathers' and Mothers' Involvement in their Children's Schools by Family Type and Resident Status. Table 1. (NCES 2001-032). Washington, DC: U.S. Dept of Education, National Center of Education Statistics, 2001.

The 1997 Gallup Youth Survey found the following among U.S. teens:

33 % live away from their father

43% of urban teens live away from their father.

Source: Youthviews, Gallup Youth Survey 4 (June, 1997).

The current hit totals on Google about fathers:

"I hate my dad" .... 8,170,000 hits

"I don't know my dad" 50,000,000 hits

"where is my dad" ......42,100,000 hits

We are living in a time in our culture where not having a quality relationship with our father has become normal. In a recent conversation with a young man in his 30s, he admitted to not having a relationship with his dad, and vowed to himself that he would be nothing like his father.

The sad thing is that as we talked, he realized that he was doing things in his life that were just like his dad. It was sobering to think that a person ended up doing the exact thing that he vowed he would never do.

As we talked, we realized that the void that he felt of not having a relationship with his father sent him down a path of self-destruction, and he hadn't even realized it until he saw himself doing the exact things his father did.

This is the story of too many people today. People are hurting from their relationships with their fathers and find themselves living their lives trying to cope with the pain, rejection, insecurity, and anger that it brings. It doesn't matter your age. Once someone has been hurt or disappointed by his or her father, it can be difficult to heal and move on in life.

Most people try to cope with the pain by forgetting about it, or by diminishing the importance of the relationship and acting like it does not matter. The problem with this is that not acknowledging the pain doesn't make the pain go away. Many people are locked in their past, and have not found a way to unlock themselves into the life that they really want.

There is good news! By the time you are finished with this book you will not only be able to be free from the pain of the past, but you will be free to walk into your future. Life is too short to live day by day coping with life. It is time to truly enjoy life, and not just endure it.

Everyone has a story. And most people, at some point in their lives, wish they could have had a better situation growing up. I remember going to school and watching other classmates, and thinking they had a perfect home. I wished I could have been born into that family. What I didn't realize is that everyone has drama. What you deal with may not be what I deal with, but, believe me, everyone is dealing with something!

The sooner I realized that I was not the only one on the planet who had things in life and at home that needed to be worked out, I was able to cope, heal, and move on into my God-given purpose. My family was not the only family that wasn't perfect. Wishing myself into another family would have resulted in having to deal with a different set of issues.

You do not have to be locked to your past anymore. You can be free, whole, complete, and positioned to do great things. You are not destined to repeat the cycles from your past. You are not destined to cope with the pain from the past for the rest of your life. Healing is available. Wholeness is available. Peace is available. Joy—yes, joy—is available to you right now.

As you read the following chapters, I would like for you to keep in mind the following things:

You are not alone. You are not the only one with issues in your past that you wish were not there.

You can't change the past. You are in one of two positions in life: either you can do something about it, or you can't. If you can't do anything about it, then stop wasting your time, energy and emotion on something that cannot change. Focusing on the past is like trying to empty the ocean with a cup; it's pointless.

Your future is up to you. Just because you have had a challenging past, doesn't mean the rest of your life is destined for struggle and pain. You choose every day the tomorrow you will have. The seed you sow today determines the harvest you wake up to tomorrow.

You are "fearfully and wonderfully made." There is not another you on the planet. No one else can do what you do. You are 100 percent original. Stop being upset about how you got here, or who got you here. Be grateful that you are here.

Make a decision to MOVE ON! You are one decision away from changing your life forever. If you don't make the decision, nothing will ever change.

Now start the journey of realization and healing, and move into the best years of your life.

"Fathers, provoke not your children to wrath."

— Ephesians 6:4

Chapter 1
Locked In Pain

"Fathers, provoke not your children to wrath." —
Ephesians 6:4

Have you ever made a list attempting to describe what you wanted in a future spouse? Have you ever predetermined certain qualities that were essential in that person based upon what you were taught or experienced in your life? And do you remember the list of things that you said to yourself that you would do as a spouse or parent when you had the opportunity? Or even the things that you said you absolutely would not do when you grew up?

It's amazing to see how much our background and upbringing shape our perception of what we want in our relationships as we grow older. Experiences, both good and bad, tend to mold our expectation of people and what we expect and need from them in our relationship.

During a national youth camp a few years ago, my wife and I had the pleasure to spend some quality time with hundreds of young people between the ages of 12 and 18.

1

Through searching for a way to address the needs, hurts and disappointments that can occur in life that impact our future relationships, we did an exercise to demonstrate the importance of not internalizing the pain from the past. We wanted to see the healing process begin in the hearts of the youth going through things in their homes that were shaping their perspective of what they would want in their future relationships.

We asked the young men and women some basic questions about their expectations in relationships. Take a moment and think about what your answer would be to the following questions:

What is your definition of a "real man/woman"?

What do you think the opposite sex is looking for in you?

What is it in your parents' relationship that you want in your marriage?

What is it in your parents' relationship that you don't want in your marriage?

WHAT IS A REAL MAN/WOMAN?

It was amazing to hear that over 95 percent of the young women believe that the first attribute of a "real man" is that he is "godly" or has a relationship with God. That was the first thing that came to mind for the young ladies when asked the question.

Other criteria included things such as knowing one's purpose, having a job, and having a place to live. Just about every young lady had these expectations as a part of their definition of a real man. They agreed that they would have a major issue with a "man" who did not have a relationship with God, did not have a job, and still lived with his parents.

They wanted a man who had a sincere relationship with God, and they wanted someone who could be the head of the home, and be a covering for their family.

Strangely enough, when we asked them about their current relationship, we got a different standard. Most of the young men that they liked, or were in a relationship with, did not have a serious relationship with God and didn't meet most of the criteria the young ladies said they wanted in a man. It was interesting to see a clear contradiction between the type of man whom they said they wanted, and whom they were actually with.

The young men, however, were not as spiritually minded or driven. The majority of the young men had set their first criteria to contain looks, or physical attractiveness. Spiritual standards were less important to the boys.

They wanted their girlfriends to look good primarily. They also wanted to feel a sense of respect for who they were, and not feel pressured into spending a lot of money on their girlfriend to make them happy.

WHAT DO YOU THINK THE OPPOSITE SEX IS LOOKING FOR IN YOU?

The answer to this question was unanimous. The young women believed the only thing the young men wanted was their bodies or sex, while the young men believed the only thing the young women wanted was money.

The young women felt pressure from the young men to be physical with them, even though it wasn't necessarily a core need of theirs. They believed that if they did not allow their boyfriend to be physically involved with them, he would move on to someone else.

This raises the following questions:

Why would the young women be willing to compromise their standards for the kind of man they wanted in a husband, and allow their bodies to be pre-maturely touched in a way that should be reserved for their future husband?

Why is it difficult for young women to adhere to their heart's desire in a man, and not settle for less?

What we discovered is what many of us deal with in our relationships, and it is usually tied to the relationship (or lack thereof) that we have with our fathers.

On the other hand, the young men in this group felt the most important quality a young lady wanted was money. If the boys didn't have money, then they believed they didn't have a chance to have a relationship with the girl they desired.

I could relate to how they felt. I remember during my rookie year in the National Football League, I met a young lady who was an alumnus from my college Penn State. We went out a couple times, and on one occasion went to the mall. While at the mall she steered me to a jewelry store and insisted that I buy a $10,000 watch. Let's just say I saved my money, and that was the last I saw of her.

Situations like that cause young men to feel that if they want a relationship with a woman, the first thing they need is money. That is not the reality of the situation. Most women want a man who has a sincere relationship with God and is not ashamed to express his love for God openly.

Later in the book we will see why there is so much confusion about what a "real man/woman" is. For now most of us, like the youth, can relate to the pressures of trying to be something we are not in order to have a relationship with someone. Any relationship that has a foundation built on a false expectation for someone to be something or someone he or she is not will have some major challenges to overcome if that relationship is going to last.

Remember, every date doesn't end in marriage, but every marriage began with a date. So be mindful of how you start your relationship.

At this point of the meeting, the youth were beginning to see that the relationships they were involved in were wrong. It was not because being in a relationship or liking someone was wrong. It was the foundation of the relationship and why they were in it in the first place that was wrong. They were beginning to see that their purpose should be clear, and in the parameters of what God ordained for a relationship to be.

They were admittedly involved with people they knew weren't their future husband or wife. But they decided to compromise their standards to be in a relationship with someone who could never meet their needs as a person.

Why waste your time? The longer you stay in a relationship with someone you know is not the person you should marry, the harder it is to break up with him or her when you need to go your separate ways. The longer you stay, the more experiences you share, and the closer the bond you establish. Before you know it, you are "stuck" in a relationship that you knew in the beginning was not supposed to last.

Typically, people stay in the relationship for the companionship and validation, not because the actual person is "the one."

Since validation is a need, the question arises, "Who is supposed to validate me?" "Who is supposed to fill the void in my heart to show me that I am valuable and worth the very best?"

The next couple of questions we asked the youth opened our eyes as to why they were in the relationships they were in, and why they compromised from the ideal standard of the person they wanted to be with.

WHAT IN YOUR PARENTS' RELATIONSHIP DO YOU WANT IN YOUR MARRIAGE?

Sadly, out of hundreds of youth at the camp, very few said something positive about the marriage they saw displayed before them in the home. It was sad to see that with so many families represented, these young people didn't see much in their parents' relationship that they wanted in their future marriages.

I think that is why TV shows like "The Cosby Show", "Family Ties", and "The Brady Bunch" were so popular. For 30 minutes we could watch a husband and wife who loved each other and worked together to raise their children. Many people wanted to experience that in their own life. The disappointing fact is that, based on the current divorce rate, and the feedback we are getting from youth, few people are actually enjoying a happy and fulfilled family environment.

This unfortunate reality is why the next question is so important in understanding the void in the hearts of so many, and why many are locked in their past hurts and disappointments of life.

WHAT IN YOUR PARENTS' MARRIAGE DO YOU NOT WANT IN YOUR MARRIAGE?

There was no shortage of information for this list. The following is a short list of things the youth observed in their homes:

Arguments

Stress

No love or romance

Financial stress, strain and lack

Broken promises

Hypocritical behavior

Although no relationship is perfect, and every relationship has ups and downs, marriage as a whole was perceived negatively by the youth. According to the youth's feedback, lack of leadership, financial hardship and a lack of love and/or romance plagued their homes. Relationships were dry, and something that they weren't chomping at the bit to become involved in themselves. Marriage is the first institution that God created, and today's youth aren't impressed with what they see.

Let's review what we have discovered thus far:

More than 95 percent of the young women we talked to felt that a "real man" had a strong relationship with God.

Most of the young men questioned listed physical appearance as the first attribute of the "ideal woman."

The young women believe young men want sex from them.

The young men believe the young women want money from them.

Few youth in the group had something positive to say about the marriage they were observing.

The majority of the youth had a negative impression of marriage due to separation, divorce, financial hardship, and a lack of romance, and lack of leadership.

Many people are struggling with their relationships today. If this is the pulse of our society, it is no wonder why divorce rates are increasing, single-parent homes are on the rise, and social Internet sites are thriving.

We all know that no relationship is perfect. Every relationship will have its disagreements from time to time, but that should be the exception, and not the rule. Homes are supposed to be a place of refuge, and refreshing from the world around us. It is in our home that we should find unconditional support and love that will help us endure the trials of life.

What these youth were experiencing was anything but that. Some of them said they don't even want to get married because they don't want to be hurt the way they saw their parents hurt each other. For others this topic began to generate some strong feelings of resentment, because in most cases, the source of the pain or stress in the home had to do with their fathers.

The more they observed turmoil in the home because of their father's absence, or his not operating in the role that God intended for him, the more resentment the youth felt toward their dad's. As a result, many of the youth had serious emotional issues and resentment due to the impact of the lack of leadership in the home.

As I observed this, it forced me to see this epidemic of fatherlessness in a whole new light. The absence of a father in a home, or a man not operating in his role, causes a destructive domino effect. It forces women and children to carry the burden of things that they were never supposed to.

I had no idea how widespread the depth

of the pain of young people of all ages experience as a result of their dads not fulfilling God's plan for their home.

There must be a solution to this epidemic. There must be a way to break the destructive cycles of neglect, hurt, disrespect, mistrust and heartbreak. If this describes the state of your relationship, keep reading, because your breakthrough is waiting for you on the other side of forgiveness.

1. What are the qualities you want in a spouse?

_____

_____

_____

   a. If you are married, does your spouse possess
     these qualities?

_____

_____

_____

   b. If you are a single adult, are these qualities the
     same as when you were a child?

_____

_____

_____

2. What experiences impacted your expectation of
   people?

_____

_____

_____

_____

_____

3. What are the most important qualities you want and need from people?

_____

_____

_____

_____

_____

4. What is your definition of a "real" man?

_____

_____

_____

_____

_____

5. What is your definition of a "real" woman?

_____

_____

_____

_____

6. What do you think that the opposite sex is looking for in you?

_____

_____

_____

_____

7. What in your parents relationship do you want in your marriage?

_____

_____

_____

_____

8. What in your parents relationship do you NOT want in your marriage?

_____

_____

_____

_____

_____

_____

"And God shall wipe away all tears from their eyes."

— Revelation 21:4a

Chapter 2
The Cry Room

"And God shall wipe away all tears from their eyes." —Revelation 21:4a

As my wife and I concluded the session, we opened the floor to the youth for an "opening to healing". We allowed them to vent anger and ask us questions as we represented people in their lives who have hurt them, and tainted their image of how God see's them.

We had the boys seated together on one side of the room, and the girls seated on the other side. I had no idea what was going to happen. My wife and I just knew that there was pain locked inside these young people that needed to be exposed.

When my wife described to me how this exercise would play out, I was thinking that the subject of family life was too sensitive for people to address. This is the type of subject that most can relate to, but no one talks about in a church setting. It is kept locked away in the family secret files of our hearts, and we never allow anyone to see what is really going on in our families, or hearts. Consequently, we all have to cope with the pain, the baggage, and the disappointments, and we have to deal with them the best way we know how, but unfortunately we carry it into future relationships through denial, anger, bitterness, or un-forgiveness.

Because this subject is so sensitive and private, I thought the youth would struggle in opening up and exposing the pain that they were feeling within themselves, but the exact opposite was true, and I couldn't have been more wrong.

It was almost as if they had been waiting for an opportunity to express what was really going on, and never had a chance to in an environment conducive for healing. Surprisingly, a young man was the first to open up, asking the first question that was addressed to me as I represented his father.

I still remember some of the questions asked of me. You might be able to identify with some of them as well:

"Dad, do you know what it felt like to have my friends show me a newspaper article with your mugshot in it and ask me, 'Hey, isn't that your father?' "

"Dad, what's wrong with me? I'm 16 years

old, and I have never heard your voice."

"Dad, why do you only go to my brother's games and not mine? Do you love him more than me?"

"Dad, I don't want your money! Why can't we just spend time together?"

"Dad, why did you show up to my graduation party drunk? I was embarrassed to be called your son."

"Dad, I HATE you! If I saw your dead body on the road, I wouldn't care. I would just keep on driving."

"Dad, why don't you care enough to be there for me?"

"Dad, how am I supposed to know how to treat a woman if you aren't there to show me?"

"Dad, the only reason I am with these boys is because I'm looking for attention from a male. And since you don't care, I'm finding the attention where I can."

It was heartbreaking to hear the hearts of so many young people who were hurting and who felt alone because of the mistakes and absence of their fathers, or absence of the role God designed for fathers I would have never known the pain and the heartache they were coping with every day.

As one person would speak up, you

could see the emotions of others boiling like a volcano about to explode. They couldn't wait for their turn to vent and share their pain.

Some of the youth were so bitter and angry they expressed it through balling up fists as they were speaking and describing wanting to inflict pain on their father as payback for hurting them. As I looked into their eyes, all I saw was anger, confusion, pain, and rejection. All I could do was let them express themselves, and trust God to give me an answer to help the young people cope with what they were going through.

There was not a dry eye in the room. The youth ended up calling it "The Cry Room" because they were touched through the unlocking of the pain in their lives and allowing themselves to be transparent and vulnerable, but open to healing. It became clear that the issues the youth expressed were the root of what the youth were enacting in their own lives.

Some of the young males were trying to figure out what a "real man" is, and the decision for some was to be with as many females as possible. They defined who they were by how many woman they could get. Since many of the young men did not have their dads guiding them towards manhood from God's perspective, they turned to multiple relationships for validation. The intent, for the most part, was not to hurt the people they were involved with, but that tended to be what happened.

The young females found themselves in one of two positions. Either they were drawn to seek love or validation through premature intimate relationships with their friends. Others had built a wall over their heart and decided to not allow themselves to be comforted emotionally by a man. A father's love was designed to nourish the emotions and ultimately build the beginning blocks of validation that would allow for wholesome friendships and relationships to be established later in life.

The feelings that were bottled up in these youth were overwhelming. The youth began to express their anger toward their parents for various reasons. Some were angry because their dad wasn't there. Others were angry because their dad wasn't living a life in a way that they could respect. Others were hurt and angry because their dad was on drugs, was unemployed, or was involved in multiple relationships with women.

21

Some were upset because their father would not spend any quality time with them. Their father was home, but would try to use gifts and/or money to make up for the lack of spending time. It was interesting to witness that the anger and pain expressed by this person was just as real and painful as someone who had no relationship with their father at all.

Some of the males in the room had no respect for their fathers because of the lifestyle their fathers choose to live. The young males especially struggled with having to watch the effects of their father's decisions on their mother. Watching their mom go through emotional and financial hardship was tough on these young men, and made it very difficult to honor or respect their father.

The young men went on to express that they had no idea what it meant to be a man, because they had no man to show them how to be one.

The young women also struggled with their own identity because of the issue with fathers. One youth wondered what was wrong with her, because she was 16 years old and had never heard her father's voice. Her father lived in the same city and knew where she lived, but for whatever reason he has never had any dialogue with his daughter. I still remember her questions: "What's wrong with me? Why am I not important enough to talk to?"

She went on to admit that the only reason she was involved in relationships with males was because she wanted to feel that she was loved by a male. And the only males in her life expressing any interest in her were the ones at school.

Some young females in the room had been so hurt by their fathers, or had witnessed the hurt their mothers were going through as a result of their fathers, that they didn't want to share their emotions, or establish close friendships with males. These young females didn't want to open themselves up to be hurt and disappointed the way they saw their mother hurt. So they felt more comfortable sharing their feelings with and being comforted by only their girlfriends.

Some of the youth are living with mothers who are coping with the fact that they have no financial, emotional, or spiritual assistance. The mothers are carrying the burden alone. The children are watching everything their moms are doing for them, as well as the struggles their moms experience. This leaves the children with only one person to point the finger to as the cause of the pain in their home—their dad.

BLENDED FAMILIES

There were other youth, now in a blended family, who had some serious issues with their stepfathers and/or mothers. I truly believe that some of these moms have been strong, have done all they could by themselves, and now have an opportunity to be loved and to receive support. However, most of the children in the room were not included in the process of the new relationship. Even when some tried to express their concern about the person their mom was about to marry, it typically fell upon deaf ears.

This causes the youth to be alienated from not only their stepfather, but also their mother. The youth felt as though there was no one in their home to talk to anymore. Therefore these young people felt they could only find an escape through their friends, the Internet, text messaging, TV, and video games. Anything was better than having to think about the situation they

Many of the youth were either having to cope with the loss of their father, or not having a close relationship with him. Now they had to cope with the loss of their mother as well.

Recently I met a grown woman who is coping with the loss of her father due to his remarriage. The father married quickly after her mother passed away, and, according to the woman, her stepmother has blocked the father from being as close to her as he used to be. All I could do was let her know that she would be okay, and to not let the decisions of her father cause a ripple effect into her life.

It is heart-breaking to think that, while grieving the loss of her mother, she is coping with losing a close relationship with her father as well. No child should feel like he or she has lost a relationship with both parents.

An interesting thing that happened at the youth camp was that the youth stopped trying to be cool in front of their friends or the opposite sex. They were sincerely honest with themselves and with one another. I found this amazing, considering the fact that youth are typically consumed with trying to be cool and to impress the opposite sex. None of that mattered. For a moment in time in their life the only thing that was important was addressing the hurt, pain, and disappointment that they had but had never addressed with anyone.

The majority of the comments of the youth were directed at me as a man in their life who was the root of the pain and anger they were feeling. It was sad to think that men had done exactly what God told fathers not to do:

"Fathers, provoke not your children to wrath" (Ephesians 6:4).

Men, knowingly or unknowingly, were hurting their children deeply by not being the men that God called them to be. Their absence in the home just compounded the problem. The number of young people who had no relationship with their fathers was staggering.

FATHERLESS, BUT THE FATHER IS THERE

There were many young people who didn't have a relationship with their father, even though their dad was in the home. Either their father's work schedule prevented them from being at home, or they never made it a priority to spend home. Either their father's work schedule prevented them from being at home, or they never made it a priority to spend quality time with their children.

Sometimes fathers think that because they are in the home and provide for the family that their job is done. That is the furthest thing from the truth. Some of the young people whose fathers were in the home yet distant emotionally or relationally, were just as hurt as a youth whose father was absent from the home, or as a youth who lives in a blended family.

These young people wanted not only the presence of their father in the home, but also a relationship with their dad. They wanted to know that they could talk to their dad and get advice and counsel when they needed it. To them, having a body in the home without having a relationship was just like not having a father.

Many of us can relate to these youth. And when we think back, we can still sense the void and pain from not having our father in our lives for whatever reason. Although all families are unique, most families are challenged with similar issues. In some we tend to hide what is really going on in our homes, and lock the feelings deep

27

within our heart. Not dealing with the issue only causes other problems in our lives, affecting either our self-esteem or our future relationships.

When given the opportunity, these youth cried out for healing, and to have their feelings acknowledged. Dealing with the reality that the person they are supposed to love, trust, and believe in isn't there for them is a reality that just doesn't make sense. These young people were screaming for the attention and love of their father. But no one has been listening. Can you imagine a newborn baby screaming to be held or changed, and no one coming to pick the baby up? What is the impact of neglect? Can one unlock the past, and breakthrough to one's destiny?

Without question, the answer is yes. As we proceed in our journey, I will address issues that both boys and girls face when it comes to relationships with their fathers. Let me tell you that even though you may be an adult, emotionally you may still feel like a boy or girl.

If you can relate to what you have just read, and if emotionally you sense that you are not healed from your past relationship with your father, then just keep reading.

Your breakthrough is a couple of chapters away.

But first ask yourself the following:

Can I relate with any of the youth?

If so, who is living or reliving my child-hood?

If I could say something to help the person reliving my childhood, what would it be?

1. Of the questions mentioned on pages 18 and 19, which impacted you the most? Discuss.

_____

_____

_____

_____

_____

2. Why is money from your father, not enough?

_____

_____

_____

_____

3. What are the issues you are facing, based on what happened in your childhood?

_____

_____

_____

_____

_____

4. Men: What was your perspective of what a real man is?

_____

_____

_____

_____

5. Do you know men who identify manhood with women and/or relationships?

_____

_____

_____

_____

6. Women: Which position do you identify with?
   a. I am drawn towards men.
   b. I have built a wall against men.
   c. All
   d. none
   Explain.

_____

_____

_____

_____

"Be ye therefore followers of God, as dear children."

— Ephesians 5:1

Chapter 3

My Hero, My Pain

"Be ye therefore followers of God, as dear children." —Ephesians 5:1

As I sat there having to be strong for the kids, I was forced to reflect on my life and my upbringing. The more I reflected on the past, the more I realized that their story is one that most people can identify with. In fact, the more research I did on the subject, the more I realized that people around the world are searching for answers about their fathers, or simply looking for a place to vent their frustrations.

Many use the Internet to do just that. In fact, when I did a Google search on the phrase "I hate my dad," more than 1,700,000 results showed up. When I searched the phrase "I don't know my dad," more than 82,000,000 results came up.

MY JOURNEY

Let me start by saying that I love my father dearly. And in no way do I want him or anyone in my family to feel embarrassed or ashamed by what happened in our family.

33

Unfortunately, there are far too many people who have similar, if not worse experiences in their home.

The purpose of this book is to let people know that they are not alone in feeling hurt or disappointed as it relates to their upbringing. Also it is to provide hope that if I was able to overcome the challenges in my upbringing, then anyone can.

I was born in Miami, Florida to a young married couple that seemed to have every-thing to look forward to in life. My parents graduated from Ivy League schools, and my father was just starting his NFL career. In fact, I am told that I was born on the same day my father scored his first touchdown, and that they almost named me "T.D."

Life was great. I remember being the most popular kid in class. Because my classmates wanted autographs of their foot-ball heroes, they all wanted to "be my friend." I had the pleasure of having my birthday parties on the Detroit Lions field, and I could go to practices on Saturdays and play hide-n-go-seek with the other kids in the team's stadium. (That wasn't always the best idea because we usually couldn't find one another.)

My father even had a Nike endorsement

contract, and I was blessed with a closet full of brand new Nikes that I could wear, and had new shoes shipped to me frequently. Life appeared to be great. From the outside looking in, nothing could be better. My dad played in the NFL, we lived in a wonderful home in the suburbs, and I was popular in school.

I had no idea that my life would go through the roller coaster of expectation and disappointment that would be instrumental in shaping my identity.

APPEARANCE IS DECEIVING

Although my family life had the potential to be the ideal situation, I was forced to wake up from my dream quickly. I realized at an early age that something was wrong in my home. Even though I had the chance to go to football games and hang out in the locker room after the game, many times I wouldn't see my father again until the day before the next game. We would go all week and not see or hear from dad.

I was only 6 or 7 years old at the time. I still remember the excitement I would get when, after not seeing Dad for days, I would hear the keys finally turn in the door, and my dad would walk through. My brother and I would run into his arms and give him the biggest hug we could. At the time I didn't care that he hadn't been there all week. I just missed my dad and was happy to see him. I didn't notice the disappointment on my mother's face as she watched us run to dad as though we were condoning his absence.

There were many Sunday mornings that my mother, brother, and I would go to church and people would always ask where my father was. I would put on my fake smile and make up something to say so they wouldn't know that I had not seen him for days, and didn't know where he was. The thought of people knowing what was actually going on in my home was embarrassing and painful. I had to put up emotional fences to guard my heart and manage my emotions.

From the outside looking in, my family appeared to be picture perfect. However, inside our house was anything but perfect.

Like most children, I thought my dad could do no wrong. I wanted to be just like him, because in my eyes he was the coolest man on the planet. Growing up, I had the chance to go to my father's football practices. I loved going into the locker room after the practice. I could get all the Gatorade and drinks I wanted, and I could meet my dad's teammates and coaches.

I eventually got my own Detroit Lions football uniform, complete with helmet, shoulder pads, and my name on the back of the jersey. I would imagine that my room was the team's locker room, and I would put on my uniform in the exact way that I saw my dad wear his. I would proceed to play an entire football game in my backyard by myself. I would throw the ball to myself, tackle myself, and even call a play in the huddle by myself. I literally reenacted what I saw my father do. I know that watching my father play football left a lasting impression on me, and a major reason why I ended up playing in the NFL myself.

Watching my father play football left a lasting impression on me, and a major reason why I ended up playing in the NFL

Transitioning from seeing my father as my inspiration to seeing him as a cause of discord and confusion in my family was difficult. It was devastating to come to understand that my dad wasn't perfect and that my parents' relationship was not what it should have been. I quickly began to understand that my father's absence in our home was not normal, and his absence started a ripple effect that my family is still feeling today.

THE SUPERHERO SYNDROME

Children are wired to believe their parents are perfect and can do anything. We want our dads to be like superheroes. We put our hope in the idea of what they are to stand for. They are to protect, provide, and come to our rescue if we ever need them. They will always be there for us when times get rough. And if we are ever scared, we can run to our hero, our dad, and he will make everything all right.

Every child wants to believe in his or her father, and rightfully so.

I have not met a child yet who doesn't have the innate desire to trust, hope, and believe in his or her dad. This is why children in school will scream at one another, insisting, "My dad is better, stronger, smarter, or richer than your dad!" Every child wants to believe in his or her father, and rightfully so. A father's role in the development of a child is vital. Our fathers help us to understand who we are, where we come from, and where we can go. Without a father, we are left to define ourselves, or allow ourselves to be defined by others.

The impact that a father has on a child is HUGE. In watching my father I was able to come to understand what I was capable of athletically. This eventually culminated into playing in the NFL myself. My career started not when I got recruited to play, but rather when I saw my father play football. I aspired to be like him and believed that I could do what he did.

Fathers tend to be like superheroes in our eyes. And like with all superheroes, our esteem of them can be diminished when we find out they have a weakness, their own version of kryptonite. I put my father on a pedestal as though he was perfect and not capable of making mistakes. But when I found out that the reality of who my father was didn't fit my perception of what I thought he was, it caused me to be confused. I couldn't understand how someone so great in my eyes could not be the person I thought. In the eyes of a child, fathers aren't supposed to have flaws, make mistakes, hurt their family, or leave their family.

FATHERS TEND TO BE LIKE SUPERHEROES IN OUR EYES

This "superhero" status we place upon our fathers usually sets us up for disappointment, and can be confusing. The thought that Dad isn't perfect just doesn't make sense. In fact, when I realized my father was not perfect, I began to view myself as though I was flawed. How else could I view myself? I thought that if my father had flaws that I must have some flaws as well.

You are wired by God to believe and have faith. Unfortunately, if you have had your trust broken as a child, it makes it difficult to trust, or develop faith in God later in life. No one wants to be hurt in the same way twice.

Read on to see how I overcame the doubts and disappointments associated with my dad, and how I unlocked myself from my past and experienced a breakthrough into my destiny.

1. Do you remember a time, when you thought your dad was cool?

_____

_____

_____

_____

_____

2. What about your father's life has made an impact on you?

_____

_____

_____

_____

_____

3. When did you realize that your dad isn't perfect?

_____

_____

_____

_____

_____

4. How did the reality of your father's imperfection impact you?

_____

_____

_____

_____

_____

5. Did you have the "super hero syndrome?"

_____

_____

_____

_____

_____

6. How has your relationship with your dad affected your relationship with God?

_____

_____

_____

_____

_____

"Thou shalt not covet thy neighbour's house."

— Exodus 20:17

Chapter 4
The Dad
I Wish I Had

"Thou shalt not covet thy neighbour's house." —Exodus 20:17

There were many days I wished that I was in a different family. I would watch shows like "The Cosby Show" and think that my family was the only one that had issues. Even my classmates appeared to have a better family than I.

I was preoccupied with being envious of things I had no control over. I also didn't understand that even if I were to switch families, I would most likely be switching my family's issues for a different set of issues. I have not found a family yet that didn't have their own set of challenges.

I was coveting their house. It appeared as though they had something that I didn't have but wanted desperately. The grass looked greener, the home seemed peaceful, and the families seemed happier. What I didn't realize is that a lot of my classmates were hurting just as much, if not more, than I was. All I knew was that there was a void, and I needed someone to fill it.

MY HIGH SCHOOL VACATION

During my freshman year of high school, a friend of mine invited me to go with him and his dad on an all-expense paid vacation to a resort in Key West, Florida. I was attending a private school with many well-off families, and this friend's family was among them.

As we flew to the resort, I recall wishing my family could do something like this someday. I especially wanted my father to be able to take time off and treat me to a trip like my friend's dad.

At the time, it seemed like it was a great vacation. We went fishing and just hung out under the sunny skies in South Florida. His dad gave us an expense account on the resort, where we could get whatever we wanted and charge it to his account. Now I must admit that it was fun to have an expense account.

As I reflect back on the trip, I don't remember my friend's dad spending a lot of quality time together with his son. We typically just hung out together and met up with his dad to let him know that we were fine. Initially, I wanted my dad to be like him. But even though he was wealthy, he didn't seem to have a great relationship with his son. What I didn't understand at the time was that money doesn't buy a close relationship with your family. It takes pressure off from having some basic needs met, but it doesn't replace wholesome communication and love.

I found myself constantly searching and reaching for normalcy. I remember feeling inferior to other classmates because of the dynamics of what was going on in my family.

RAM IN THE BUSH

Although my family experience was hard emotionally, the thing that got me through the difficult times was the fact that my mother found a good church for us to attend. This was critical in my development as a young man. There I was taught the word of God. In spite of everything that was going on around me, I knew that God still loved me and had a plan for my life.

We not only had a church that taught the word of God, but also had a pastor who lived the word. There are many churches in the world today. But how many have leaders that live what they teach? This is one of the issues the young people at the youth camp had with their parents—living with a double standard.

Just like watching my father play football left an impression on me, observing the life of a godly man also left a mark that couldn't be erased. Bishop Keith Butler, pastor and founder of Word of Faith International Christian Center, happened to be the pastor my mother found. And my life would never be the same.

I still remember the first time I heard Bishop Butler quote a verse of the Bible without reading it. I'm not talking about something familiar like John 3:16 or Psalms 23. He quoted the verse, and I immediately opened the Bible to see if he quoted the scripture correctly.

I was about 6 years old at the time. I had never heard anyone quote Scripture like that before. I said to myself that I wanted to be able to quote scriptures like that someday. As I observed him, I was able to see the possibility of the type of man I could become. I did not have to be separated from my wife and children when I grew up. I could be a man that pleased God.

I soon made a decision to become the dad I wish I had. But in order to accomplish this goal, I needed to get the keys to unlock myself from the bondage of my past, and understand the necessary principles to live by that would allow me to break-through to my destiny.

Are you ready to get your keys to unlock yourself from your past? Then turn the page.

1. Did you ever wish you were in a different family?

_____

_____

_____

_____

_____

2. Did it make you feel guilty? Explain.

_____

_____

_____

_____

_____

3. Did you have any other men in your life that you
   looked up to?

_____

_____

_____

_____

_____

_____

4. Who were those men?

_____

_____

_____

_____

_____

5. Who's life influenced what you wanted to be?

_____

_____

_____

_____

_____

6. How did the process impact your expectation of others?

_____

_____

_____

_____

_____

"For I know the thoughts that I think toward you, saith the Lord, thoughts of peace, and not of evil, to give you an expected end."

— Jeremiah 29:11

Chapter 5
Lock... Lock...
Who's There?

"For I know the thoughts that I think toward you, saith the Lord, thoughts of peace, and not of evil, to give you an expected end."
—Jeremiah 29:11

Avoiding the source or cause of pain will not make the pain go away. We can't keep going to sleep hoping that we will wake up to a new situation. Once I realized I had some real issues that needed to be dealt with, I was able to know what I needed God to heal within me.

Denial only delays deliverance. And whining or complaining is like sitting in a rocking chair: it gives you the feeling of moving, but you are not going anywhere. This is where too many people are today. They are complaining about what's wrong in their life, and wallowing in the mud of life, rather than seeking how to not allow the pain to keep them in bondage anymore.

When my father and mother separated, there were many difficult nights when I could hear my mother crying in her room. I found myself having to be strong for her and my brother. I tried the best I could to keep a level head about the situation.

As I reflect on it, there is one thing I can put my finger on that gave me the ability to be strong and not be in bondage to what was going on around me: my personal relationship with Jesus Christ.

I learned through the teaching of God's word that it was not the perfect will of God for my family to experience any hardship. The things we experienced were the direct results of the decisions of my parents in their relationship, and it had nothing to do with God's will for our home.

I even got to the place where I was able to isolate what was going on in my home from what I needed to do to prepare myself for school and sports. I remember the Lord dealing with me about this when I was in high school. He asked me some simple questions:

"What does your father's not being home have to do with you studying for tests and doing your homework?"

"What does your father's not being home have to do with you catching a football?"

"What does your parents' relationship have to do with you and My plans for your life?"

The answer to all of these questions is NOTHING. Although these things were realities in my life, none of them had anything to do with my doing what God told me to do. I can tell you what each one of those issues were . . . EXCUSES.

EXCUSES

"And the man said, The woman whom thou gavest to be with me, she gave me of the tree, and I did eat." (Genesis 3:12)

Since the Garden of Eden and the Fall of mankind, human beings have attempted to come up with an excuse as to why we have not done what God commanded us to do. It's easier to accept where we are in life if we have a legitimate excuse as to why we are not more successful than we are.

People typically don't like taking accountability for the decisions they make in life. Consequently, we tend to shift blame to others as to why we do what we do. Having a poor relationship with a father gives people an excuse to live with, and sometimes they carry that excuse into other areas of their life.

Even some of the young girls at the youth camp tried to justify the relationships they were in, saying it was because of their father. I ask the question, What does your father's not being home have to do with your being engaged in premarital sex, or your being involved in a relationship that God clearly says not to? The answer again is "Nothing."

I am not saying that there are not emotional issues that need to be addressed. But what I am saying is that the way we need to address these issues must be in the light of the word of God. If we don't follow God's word then we will be causing more heartache and disappointment by trying to solve our problems our way. And when we try to fix something that only God can fix, we tend to make a mess of things.

Your trying to fix a broken heart is like your trying to fix the engine of a space shuttle. The only people capable of doing a diagnostic assessment on what is wrong with it are the people who made it. If I tried to fix it, I would undoubtedly make it worse rather than better. Why? Because I have no clue about how it's supposed to work;

because I didn't make it. Sure, I could tinker around and tighten a bolt here, and bang a hammer there, but I would be ignorant of what truly needs to be done in order for the engine to work properly.

Your heart is no different. When we try to fix the pain in our heart with other relationships, we only make a bad situation worse. When we are hurt emotionally, we tend to put too much emphasis on another person to meet our needs. And whenever that person does something that reminds us of someone who hurt us in the past, we tend to take the pain and anger of the past out on that person.

Instead of trying to fix ourselves or look to other people to fix or heal our emotional wounds, we must go to the One who made our hearts, and allow Him to heal and fix what is broken.

Did you realize that your heart is so important to God that you are one of the specific people that God sent Jesus to minister to? In Luke 4:18 Jesus says, "The Spirit of the Lord is upon me, because he hath anointed me to preach the gospel to the poor; he hath sent me to heal the brokenhearted."

Think about that for a moment. The God

of creation is so mindful of you and what you are going through emotionally that He "sent" Jesus specifically to heal what you are going through right now.

I want you to know how valuable you are to God. In this passage you see the Trinity of God directly involved in making sure you were healed from the pain of your past. You see the Father in this passage because He "sent" Jesus. You see the Son making a declaration about why He was sent, and to whom He was sent. And you see the Holy Spirit giving Jesus a specific anointing to "heal the brokenhearted."

Don't be deceived into thinking that God is not mindful of you. God can't stop thinking about you. He is so mindful that He doesn't want you to have to endure another moment of a broken heart. God wants you whole and complete and totally set free from the pain of your past. You don't have to wait another moment for your BREAKTHROUGH.

1. What decisions are you willing to make in order
   to get a different outcome in your family?

_____

_____

_____

_____

_____

2. What areas in your life will you study to be
   empowered to make better decisions?

_____

_____

_____

_____

_____

3. Are you willing to exchange your past for God's
   future?

_____

_____

_____

_____

_____

"What is man,
that thou art mindful
of him? and the son
of man, that thou
visitest him?"

— Psalms 8:4

Chapter 6
What's My Value?

"What is man, that thou art mindful of him? and the son of man, that thou visitest him?"
—Psalms 8:4

We have now come to a place of understanding the legitimate pain and insecurity that many people are struggling with today. You may have wondered for years about your purpose and what is your overall value. If you did not receive love and acceptance from your father, then it is very difficult to view yourself with esteem and self-worth.

This is why people are starving for attention and acceptance in our society today. Social networks like MySpace, Facebook, and Twitter are ever expanding because people are longing to be connected.

Gang activity is increasing in our schools because gangs are portraying themselves to be a family that will always be there for the youth—even to the death. This would be appealing to someone who is struggling with self-worth and feels alone in his or her own family. It's sad to say that in today's society gang members show more commitment to one another than some married couples do.

The absence of a father's love causes a domino effect we can see in every aspect of our culture.

But what if I told you that you could receive a Father's love today. What if you had a Father who would always be there, and would never let you down? What if you had a Father who loved you so much that you were always on His mind, and He was always looking for ways to be a blessing to you?

Does it sound too good to be true? It's not. God loves you that much. Perhaps you're thinking, God?! If God loved me so much, then why did He allow this to happen to me? Why was I born into this family? Why didn't He stop what was going on in my family? If God loved me so much, then why did He let my heart be broken?

These are excellent questions and concerns. And most people are mad not only at their natural fathers but also at God, because they blame Him for what has happened to them. This is no different than what Adam did in the Garden when he said "the woman that you gavest me."

Basically, Adam was saying that if God had not given him this woman, Adam would not be in the situation that he was in. Similarly, many people feel that if God had not put them in the families they are in their lives would be better today.

Well, let's address this issue head on because it is the key to unlocking your past and breaking through to the destiny God has for you.

WHY DID GOD "LET" THIS HAPPEN?

As we address this issue, let's look at the story of Creation a different way. Let's try to answer the question "What is it about God's nature that compelled Him to make the statement in Genesis 2:18—it is not good for man to be alone"?

As we look at this we will discover that there is a design God intended. But if we don't understand the design and plan that He intended from the beginning, then we can mess it up quickly. Mankind has the capacity to turn something that is supposed to be wonderful and good into something that is a source of pain and bondage. Therefore, we must understand the "whys" of God in order to flow in harmony with His plan.

Why did God say it is not good for man to be alone? When we look at the account in Genesis 1, we see that everything God did was "good." The entire first chapter of

Genesis is filled with God creating and immediately looking at His creation and saying "It is good."

What was it about Adam that caused God to stop what He was doing and make a declarative statement about man? Let's again look at what God said: "It is not good that the man should be alone" (Genesis 2:18). God was not saying that Adam was not good; God was making a point that mankind should not be alone, that we need companionship.

Why is companionship so important to God? Because God Himself is relational and exists to interact socially with Himself (the Trinity) and mankind. Notice in Genesis 1:26, God the Father talks to God the Son and the Holy Spirit in deciding to make man. God says, "Let us make man." When God the Father created, He did it in 100 percent harmony with the entire Trinity.

It was God who initiated the conversation with man and enjoyed spending time with man in the "cool of the day." In Genesis chapter 3, it is God who looked for Adam and asked him what he did. It is God who initiated relationships throughout the Bible. Here is a short list of scriptures showing God's involvement and desire to be involved in the lives of mankind.

IS GOD INVOLVED?

God looks for Adam:

"And they heard the voice of the Lord God walking in the garden in the cool of the day: and Adam and his wife hid themselves from the presence of the Lord God amongst the trees of the garden. And the Lord God called unto Adam, and said unto him, Where art thou?" (Genesis 3:8-9)

God initiates a relationship with Abraham:

Now the Lord had said unto Abram, Get thee out of thy country, and from thy kindred, and from thy father's house, unto a land that I will shew thee: And I will make of thee a great nation, and I will bless thee, and make thy name great; and thou shalt be a blessing." (Genesis 12:1-2)

God comes to deliver the children of Israel:

"I am the God of thy father, the God of Abraham, the God of Isaac, and the God of Jacob. And Moses hid his face; for he was afraid to look upon God. And the Lord said, I have surely seen the affliction of my people which are in Egypt, and have heard their cry by reason of their taskmasters; for I know their sorrows; And I am come down to deliver them out of the hand of the Egyptians, and to bring them up out of that land unto a good land and a large, unto a land flowing with milk and honey." (Exodus 3:6-8b)

GOD INHABITS THE PRAISES OF HIS PEOPLE:

"It came even to pass, as the trumpeters and singers were as one, to make one sound to be heard in praising and thanking the Lord; and when they lifted up their voice with the trumpets and cymbals and instruments of music, and praised the Lord, saying, For he is good; for his mercy endureth for ever: that then the house was filled with a cloud, even the house of the Lord; So that the priests could not stand to minister by reason of the cloud: for the glory of the Lord had filled the house of God." (2 Chronicles 5:13-14)

GOD BECAME FLESH:

"In the beginning was the Word, and the Word was with God, and the Word was God. The same was in the beginning with God. . . . And the Word was made flesh, and dwelt among us, (and we beheld his glory, the glory as of the only begotten of the Father,) full of grace and truth." (John 1:1-2, 14)

GOD SENT JESUS OUT OF HIS LOVE FOR US:

"For God so loved the world, that he gave his only begotten Son, that whosoever believeth in him should not perish, but have everlasting life." (John 3:16)

GOD WANTS YOU WHERE HE IS:

"In my Father's house are many mansions: if it were not so, I would have told you. I go to prepare a place for you. And if I go and prepare a place for you, I will come again, and receive you unto myself; that where I am, there ye may be also." (John 14:2-3)

GOD SENT HIS SPIRIT TO
LIVE WITH YOU FOREVER:

"And I will pray the Father, and he shall give you another Comforter, that he may abide with you forever; even the Spirit of truth; whom the world cannot receive, because it seeth him not, neither knoweth him: but ye know him; for he dwelleth with you, and shall be in you. I will not leave you comfortless: I will come to you." (John 14:16-18)

It has been the plan of God from the beginning to have a relationship with us. You are so important to God that He wants to live in you.

"For ye are the temple of the living God; as God hath said, I will dwell in them, and walk in them; and I will be their God, and they shall be my people." 2 Corinthians 6:16)

By receiving Jesus Christ as your personal Lord and Savior, you allow God to move in, heal you from your past, and begin a relationship with Him as your Father. He also gives you His Spirit to abide in you to help you through the storms of life.

God has never changed His mind about you. From the very beginning, God has been moving in an effort to reveal Himself to the world.

It's not good for mankind to be alone because it is not the nature of God to be alone. He wants a relationship with you, and made you to desire a relationship with him and with people around you.

Remember, the family is the first institution God made, and every other relationship or institution is built upon the foundation of the family. God's plan from the beginning is still His plan today. His plan is to bless you and cause you to prosper through a family that has a relationship with Him.

WHY DID GOD LET THIS HAPPEN?

Many people misunderstand the sovereignty of God. God is all-powerful, all-knowing, and ever-present. However, God does not make mankind do anything. God gave us free will to choose to have a relationship with Him or not.

God did not make Adam eat the fruit of the tree. Adam chose to eat from it, knowing the consequences of his decision. We too make our own decisions and are forced to live with the consequences of those decisions. God has revealed in His word what He would like for us to do, but ultimately it is up to us.

DEUTERONOMY 30:19 STATES:

"I call heaven and earth to record this day against you, that I have set before you life and death, blessing and cursing: therefore choose life, that both thou and thy seed may live."

We have been given the freedom to choose. Think of it this way: God was not the one who made the person decide to hurt you. Ask yourself, "Have I ever hurt someone else, knowingly or unknowingly?" More than likely you have hurt someone else with a decision you made. Would it be fair for the person you hurt to blame God for your decision? Of course not. God did not tell you to cheat on your spouse, girlfriend, or boyfriend. God did not tell you to gamble your mortgage payment, or say something hurtful during an argument.

I remember a scene in the movie "The Usual Suspects" in which at the end of the movie Kevin Spacey says, "The greatest trick the devil ever pulled was convincing the world that he didn't exist." That is so true. God is blamed for everything. Whether it is natural disasters, family disputes, or heartbreak, God has been blamed for it all. God is the One who is reaching out to heal you from your past, not the One causing the pain.

Here is an interesting promise from God found in Isaiah 54:4:

"Fear not; for thou shalt not be ashamed: neither be thou confounded; for thou shalt not be put to shame: for thou shalt forget the shame of thy youth, and shalt not remember the reproach of thy widowhood any more."

What God has in store for you is so great that He desires for you to forget the pain of your past. I can honestly say this is true for me. Many times I have to try to remember what took place during my upbringing because I am not in bondage to it anymore. God has caused me to forget the shame of my youth.

I have been set free from the pain and hurt because I understand that it was not God who made the situation, but that it was the result of individual decisions that my parents made in their relationship.

Lastly, let's drive this point home. How many children are born out of wedlock every day? Did God tell that man and woman who were not married to have intercourse? Of course not. God will never tell someone to do something that will violate His word. The two individuals made a decision to have intercourse, and the result of it was conception. Many times the parents were not intending to have a child, but they were caught up in the moment.

The child is then born, but sometimes the relationship of the parents was not developed enough to be able to have a strong, lasting, and loving marriage. Too many times the dynamics of the relationship were only physical, and not something that is productive toward a marriage that will stand the test of time.

Would it be fair for the child that came from their relationship to blame God? No, because God was not the one who told the parents to have intercourse outside of marriage. God did not want that child to not have a father, or for their parents to struggle financially because of the decisions that were made.

MORE FOOD FOR THOUGHT:

Did God make you go in debt?

Did God tell you to buy a car that you really couldn't afford?

Did God tell you to buy a house that you could get approved for but was not in your budget?

Did God tell you to date that person who hurt you?

If we are honest with ourselves, we will see that God gets a black eye for many of the things that are clearly the results of our own choices. God is not the source or cause of our problems. But He is the source of the solution.

It is our responsibility to trust that He will do what He said He would do. Trust that your situation did not catch Him by surprise. Although He did not want the people to hurt you, He provided a way for you to receive the healing you would need to unlock your past and step into your destiny.

If you are a father reading this now I can't express to you how important you are to your family and children. Regardless, of what may have happened in the past, or the time that may have been lost, your ability to go to your children and let them know how much you love and care about them will help to heal some of their pain that has been caused by our mistakes.

James 1:5 states, "If any of you lack wisdom, let him ask of God, that giveth to all men liberally, and upbraideth not; and it shall be given him."

If you need wisdom to be the husband or father that you desire to be, simply ask God for the wisdom to be who God has called you to be. You are made to hear from God, and to be the leader and covering for your home and family. I encourage you to step up, and step into your role.

CAST YOUR CARE

First Peter 5:7 states, "Casting all your care upon him; for he careth for you."

God loves you so much that he doesn't want you trying to figure out how to deal with the cares of your life. He commands us to cast the care on Him, because He cares for us. God loves you so much that He chose to not live without you.

That's right! You are so valuable to God that He chose to not live without you. God is eternal; He always was and always will be. He is the Alpha and the Omega, the beginning and the end. When Adam sinned in the Garden, God chose to not leave us in a fallen state. God chose to do whatever it took to win us back to Himself.

When did He make that decision? He did it before the foundation of the world.

Ephesians 1:4-5 reads, "According as he hath chosen us in him before the foundation of the world, that we should be holy and without blame before him in love: having predestinated us unto the adoption of children by Jesus Christ to himself, according to the good pleasure of his will."

I want you to notice a couple things in this passage of scripture: God chose you before the foundation of the world.

God chose to adopt you according to the good pleasure of His will.

POINT #1: CHOSEN

Let's break this down a little more. When God chose you before the foundation of the world, He predetermined your value to Himself. He decided that He wanted you to be holy and without blame in His presence, experiencing His love. This was His plan before He said "Let there be light."

Another thing we must understand about God is that He cannot change. The Amplified version of Hebrews 6:17-18 reads: "Accordingly God also, in His desire to show more convincingly and beyond doubt, to those who were to inherit the promise, the unchangeableness of His purpose and plan, intervened (mediated) with an oath. This was so that by two unchangeable things (His promise and His oath), in which it is impossible for God ever to prove false or deceive us, we who have fled (to Him) for refuge might have mighty indwelling strength and strong encouragement to grasp and hold fast the hope appointed for us and set before (us)."

God made an oath to Himself to watch over His promise to you. God has never stopped thinking about you. And even as God is inspiring me to write this book, God is thinking about you right now. God knew that you would be reading these pages. How you found this book was not an accident, but rather an opportunity for God to let you know how much He truly loves you.

POINT #2: ADOPTION

We just read in Ephesians that God wants to adopt you. In an adoption the parents choose a child to engraft into their home and give the child the same rights and privileges as a biological child. You are so precious to God that He chose to make you a part of His family.

Now that's great news! For it means that even if my earthly father has failed me, I can have a relationship with my heavenly Father that will make up the difference.

Paul writes a prayer in Ephesians 3:14-19 that I pray for you now: "For this cause I bow my knees unto the Father of our Lord Jesus Christ, of whom the whole family in heaven and earth is named, that he would grant you, according to the riches of his glory, to be strengthened with might by his Spirit in the inner man; that Christ may dwell in your hearts by faith; that ye, being rooted and grounded in love, may be able to comprehend with all saints what is the breadth, and length, and depth, and height; and to know the love of Christ, which passeth knowledge, that ye might be filled with all the fulness of God."

God not only wants you to be a part of His family, but He also wants you to know the breadth, length, depth, and height of His love for you.

I don't know about you, but that would be good enough if it ended there. But it doesn't. The passage goes on to say that God desires that you be filled with the fullness of His presence. Does this sound like a God that doesn't love? Of course not. God has been waiting all eternity for you.

The question is are you going to allow Him to come into your life, establish a relationship with Him, and let Him heal your broken heart?

1. Why is acceptance and validation from your father important?

_____

_____

_____

_____

_____

2. Did you ever question God's love for you because of what was happening in your home?

_____

_____

_____

_____

3. Based on what you have read, what was God's involvement in your home?

_____

_____

_____

_____

_____

4. Do believe that God wants a relationship with you? Discuss.

_____

_____

_____

_____

_____

5. Why did God let bad things happen in your family?

_____

_____

_____

_____

_____

6. What caused the drama in my upbringing? How can it be fixed?

_____

_____

_____

_____

_____

"And their sins and iniquities will I remember no more."

— Hebrews 10:17

Chapter 7

Stopping Destructive Cycles

"And their sins and iniquities will I remember no more." —Hebrews 10:17

*I*n the beginning of the book I told you about a young man who did not have a relationship with his father and who vowed to himself that he would never do what his father did. He found himself later in life doing some of the same things his father did. This realization was upsetting because in his heart he really did not want to repeat the same destructive cycles of his father.

There may be many of you who find yourself in a similar situation. Some men find themselves not wanting to make the same mistakes of their father, but end up struggling with similar issues. Whether it is alcoholism, drug abuse, unfaithfulness, or incarceration, many men find it difficult to break the pattern of destruction.

There are women who find themselves

not wanting to be in a relationship with a man who is like their father, but somehow end up attracted to men with similar characteristics. Ultimately, this leads to broken hearts, and failed relationships.

While growing up I used to fear that I would make the same mistakes my father did. That is, until I found these promises from God about generational curses:

"Now, lo, if he beget a son, that seeth all his father's sins which he hath done, and considereth, and doeth not such like, . . . hath executed my judgments, hath walked in my statutes; he shall not die for the iniquity of his father, he shall surely live. . . . The soul that sinneth, it shall die. The son shall not bear the iniquity of the father . . . the righteousness of the righteous shall be upon him. . . . But if the wicked will turn from all his sins that he hath committed, and keep all my statutes, and do that which is lawful and right, he shall surely live, he shall not die. . . . Have I any pleasure at all that the wicked should die? saith the Lord God: and not that he should return from his ways, and live?" (Ezekiel 18:14-23)

God gives us great news: we are not destined to be punished for the sins of our fathers. We must consider the paths that our fathers took and make a decision to follow God's instruction, instead of our fathers' examples. God's instruction will always lead you to life and peace.

"This book of the law shall not depart out of thy mouth; but thou shalt meditate therein day and night, that thou mayest observe to do according to all that is written therein: for then thou shalt make thy way prosperous, and then thou shalt have good success." (Joshua 1:8)

If we observe and do God's word, we can have success in every area of our lives. The passage in Ezekiel 18 states that we will not pay for the mistakes of our fathers. All we have to do is to choose to do things God's way.

I have found this to be true in my life. I could have gone down the pathway that would have ended in divorce, and multiple children outside of my marriage, but I decided to act on God's word in my life and not give into any thoughts or feelings that were contrary to what God would have me to do.

It is not always easy. But the more I stay in God's word, and submitted to God's authority in the earth, the more I am able to grow and experience peace in my home.

Through the light of God's word, I have been able to choose God's way—the path of life and blessing, rather than the path of death and cursing. I know that if I am able to do it, by God's grace, then anyone can, because what God does for one person He is willing to do for everyone.

The last part of Ephesians 6:9 states: "...knowing that He Who is both their Master and yours is in heaven, and that there is no respect of persons (no partiality) with Him."

He will bless your life if you choose to act on His word.

Your father's mistakes are just that, his mistakes. You don't have to live another day in fear of making the same mistakes, or in the pain of the past. God wants you to know that He sent Jesus to set you totally free.

Now it's time to start fresh and have your new beginning.

"Therefore if any man be in Christ, he is new creature: old things are passed away; behold, all things are become new."

— 2 Corinthians 5:17

Chapter 8
New Beginnings

"Therefore if any man be in Christ, he is new creature: old things are passed away; behold, all things are become new."
—2 Corinthians 5:17

We have discovered that in spite of what you have been through growing up, and the disappointment that you may have experienced, that God loves you deeply and wants to heal your broken heart. Regardless of how long it has been since you were hurt, God is able to heal you and allow you to break free from the pain of your past once and for all.

It is time to walk in the fullness of God's best for you. It's time to stop enduring life, and time to start enjoying it. Jesus came so that you can have an abundant life now. A life full of peace and joy is available to you right now. All you have to do is receive what God has already done for you.

How? You receive by simply asking God in prayer. Prayer is simply communication with God, who would love to hear your voice. Jesus is quoted saying in Mark 11:24:

"Therefore I say unto you, What things soever ye desire, when ye pray, believe that ye receive them, and ye shall have them."

What are you believing God for? Is it healing of a past hurt or emotional scar that has followed you throughout your life? Or, do you need restoration of a broken relationship that needs mending? Whatever it is, believe that you receive and you will have it.

Many of you, even as you are reading these pages, will experience the presence of God coming into your room, and a supernatural peace that passes understanding. God will manifest Himself as a confirmation that He is mindful of you and desires to dwell in your life.

Simply ask Him to heal you. First John 5:13-15 states:

"These thing have I written unto you that believe on the name of the Son of God; that ye may know that ye have eternal life, and that ye may believe on the name of the Son of God. And this is the confidence that we have in him, that, if we ask any thing according to his will, he heareth us: and if we know that he hear us, whatsoever we ask, we know that we have the petitions that we desired of him."

This passage of scripture guarantees that God will answer your prayer and grant you your petitions. But there is one condition: Do you believe on the name of the Son of God, Jesus Christ? Do you believe that God loved you enough to send Jesus to pay the price of sin that you could not pay? Do you believe that God raised Jesus after being crucified for you, and who is seated at the right hand of God? Do you believe that Jesus is "the Way, the Truth, and the Life" and that and no one can come to the Father accept through Him?

If so, your breakthrough and healing is almost here. Repeat the following prayer. Say it out loud where you can hear yourself talk. Do not just read it. Communicate with God. He has been waiting for you.

REPEAT THIS PRAYER

"Heavenly Father, in the name of Jesus, I believe that Jesus Christ is the Son of God. I believe He died for me at Calvary and that You raised Him from the dead. Lord Jesus, come into my heart now; come into my life now and save me. I choose to turn away from sin, and turn my life to You.

"Father, You said that You sent Jesus to heal the broken-hearted. I ask You now to heal my heart and fill me with Your peace, love, and joy. I choose to forgive the person/people who hurt me, and ask that you move in their life, the way you are moving in mine now. Thank You for hearing my prayer and for answering my prayer. Thank You for moving in my life now. I ask this in Jesus' name. Amen."

Now begin to thank God for what He has just done for you. Thank Him for hearing your prayer and for answering your prayer. Thank Him for healing your heart and adopting you into His family. Thank Him for being mindful of you, even when you weren't mindful of Him. Just continue to thank God.

[Note: Please stop reading at this point and spend some time thanking God for what He is doing in your life and heart right now. Note what happens when you pray, and thank God.]

CONGRATULATIONS!

You have just made the most important decision of your life. You have allowed yourself to establish a relationship with God, and allowed God to move in your life. God wants to show you His love for you and to be a father to you that will never let you down.

Please make sure you find a good church to teach you the word of God. Also contact one of the many support organizations that are in place to assist you in any way they can.

Go to www.thedadiwishihad.com and join the list of people who have allowed God to unlock the chains that once had them bound. You can subscribe to our blog and submit what God is doing in your life. This way you can encourage someone else who may be going through what you went through.

I am so excited about your future. Your best life begins NOW.

Chapter 9
My Dad and Me Today

I am honored to say that my dad and I have a good relationship today! I have access to him when I need him, and he was even very supportive of this book. I am honored to call him my dad and I appreciate all that he is for me today.

All relationships are works in progress, and they all have ups and downs. I have learned to appreciate the fact that life is too short to dwell on things that in the long run don't matter. I have the opportunity now to enjoy time and conversation with my dad, and I plan on maximizing my opportunity.

I also want to thank my father-in-law and pastor, Henry Coles, Jr., who has opened his home and heart to me. He truly has helped me understand what it means to be a husband and father, but even more than that he showed me how to live by faith. Bishop Butler truly taught me faith, but God blessed me with an opportunity to watch a person live by faith day, by day.

You never know who is watching you, and will need to learn how to be the person God has called them to be by just watching you. Everything we do in life is a seed. And I encourage all of us to be mindful of what we are sowing in the lives of those around us. I was blessed to have people to sow the right seed, to produce the right harvest in my life today.

I encourage you that if you are a father that has not been there for your children the way you desired to be, it is not too late. Please reach out to your family and let them know how much you care. Start sowing the right seed for your family today!

If you are a child who is still longing for a relationship with your dad, please continue to pray for him. And if an opportunity comes to re-establish a relationship with him, jump through the door of opportunity!

God knows where we are now. He also knows what we need now. God knows how to get you your "ram in the bush" (Exodus 3:2-3)

It is NOT too late!